Inculturating Liturgy in Sri Lanka:

Contextualization in the Church of Ceylon

by Phillip Tovey (ed.)
and
Rasika Abeysinge
Marc Billimoria
Keerthisiri Fernando
Narme Wickremesinghe

The sanctuary of Christ Church Baddegama. The cover picture is of Trinity College Chapel Kandy, both © Phillip Tovey.

ISSN: 0951-2667
ISBN: 978-0-334-05966-0

Contents

1
Introduction

Phillip Tovey

The Church of Ceylon is two dioceses extra-provincial to Canterbury but governed by a single General Assembly (synod). It has a rich history of inculturation of the liturgy. This story is not well known, and the purpose of this book is to tell the story to the rest of the Anglican Communion and the wider church. Sri Lanka has a unique mixture of cultures and religions, Buddhist and Hindu, in which the Christian church has developed. There has also been a context of strong socialist ideology. It is in this context that the church lives. Is the church to be in a westernised form requiring people to abandon their culture, if they wish to become Christians? This question has been wrestled with for almost a century. Out of religious and ideological dialogue the church has developed liturgical forms that help shape Sri Lankan Christians (rather than Christians in Sri Lanka). This has been fostered from the 1930s by some exceptional Christian leaders who took bold steps to contextualise worship. These include Lakdasa de Mel, Lakshman Wickremesinghe, Yohan Devananda and Vijaya Vidyasagara. The Ceylon Liturgy of 1931 was one of the first liturgies to be written by Sri Lankans and incorporate inculturation as a basic philosophy. This book tells the story of these developments.

The next chapter sets the context. In order to examine the liturgies an understanding of the context is required. It is written by two authors. Keerthisiri Fernando is bishop of Kurunegala and a noted sociologist. Rasika Abeysinge is a priest and school chaplain with several books published on social context. Together they explain the cultural background for liturgical development.

The third chapter is by Phillip Tovey, an international liturgical scholar and a priest and Principal of the Local Ministry Pathway in the Diocese of Oxford. It examines the development of the Ceylon Liturgy and its influence in the current eucharistic rites of the Church of Ceylon.

The fourth chapter is by Marc Billimoria, who is a priest and Warden (Principal) of S. Thomas' College, Mt. Lavinia on the outskirts of Colombo. It looks at the liturgies developed by Yohan Devananda and The Christian Workers Fellowship. The first is the New World Liturgy and the second is the Workers' Mass. Both have influenced official texts and been seed grounds for developing inculturation.

The fifth and final chapter is by Narme Wickremesinghe, a retired Consultant in Occupational Medicine who has served in the Church of Ceylon Liturgical Committee from 1976 to the present day and was its Chair when the inculturated liturgies were approved by the Episcopal Synod and General Assembly. It looks at the way inculturation is a part of the present liturgies of the Church of Ceylon.

We make this rich story of inculturation in Sri Lanka available to the rest of the Communion in the hope that others will be encouraged to take steps appropriate to their context.

2

The Sri Lankan Context: History & Social Setting and the Church's Attitudes to Local Cultures, Religions, Ideologies

Keerthisiri Fernando and Rasika Abeysinghe

Introduction

Sri Lanka is an island country in South Asia in the Indian Ocean. Sri Lanka's prehistory is dated from 125,000 years ago and its documented history has a span of over 3000 years (Deraniyagala: 1996). The origin of Buddhism is well documented within the history of the country, with the Pali Canon (Collection of Scriptures in the Pali Language of Theravada Buddhism) being written in 29 BC at the fourth Buddhist Council held in Sri Lanka. (Gonda: 1983, 10). Indigenous tribes (Yaksha, Naga and Veddahs) were its original inhabitants and with the arrival of a prince from India, called Vijaya, Sri Lanka's monarchical rule was established. (Mahavansa: 2007).

Sri Lanka's kingdom shifted from the North Central regions towards the central regions over 1900 years (380 BC -1515 AD). Sri Lanka was colonized by the Portuguese (1505-1656), the Dutch (1656-1796) and the British (1796-1815). In 1948 Sri Lanka declared independence from the British Crown and became a republic in 1972. Today it has a semi presidential system of governance. (De Silva: 1981, 133-210)

Its export economy is based on tea, rice, clothing and tourism. Sri Lanka is rated high on the Human Development Index and is top ranked in terms of per capita income among the South Asian countries. Sri Lanka has a rich mix of ethnicity (Sinhalese 74.8%, Sri Lankan and Indian Tamils 16% and Moors 9.2% with small populations of Malays and Burghers), and religions (Buddhists 70%, Hindu 13%, Islam 9.2% and Christians 7.4%) (Department of Census and Statistics: 2012).

Christianity in Sri Lanka

It is widely believed that Christianity began in Sri Lanka in the first century. This is attributed to the apostle Thomas, who is also the patron saint of the land, who according to legend preached in Sri Lanka and a church in Gintupitiya in the Colombo suburbs is named after him. Records suggest that Christians in Kerala (also evangelized by St Thomas) and Christians of the Church of the East existed in Sri Lanka even before the advent of western powers in the 16th century (Aprem: 2013). The location of Sri Lanka continuously brought traders from other parts of the world who contributed to the continuation and enrichment of the faith. One fact that has been pointed to in the search for Christianity before the colonizers has been the 6th century Persian Cross which was found in Anuradhapura (Hocart: 1924, 51-52).

When the Portuguese invaded Sri Lanka, there were numerous conversions to Roman Catholicism such that even today almost 83% of all Christian faith adherents in the land are Roman Catholics. The Dutch mission in the 17th century was able to convert almost 21% of the population to Christianity. They also built the first Protestant church of the country in Wolvendhal in Galle in 1749 (Paranavithana: 2002). This number has gradually decreased, which is attributed to the absence of the vivid sense of worship with the stimulation of the five senses that was present in the Roman Catholic rite.

When the British came to Sri Lanka several denominations arrived, primarily Anglicans, Methodists, Baptists, Presbyterians, Salvation

Army and the American Ceylon Mission. Anglican mission was mainly through the work of the Church Missionary Society and the Society for the Propagation of the Gospel (Balding: 1922, 63-68). Today these denominations belong to the National Christian Council and several independent churches form the National Christian Evangelical Alliance of Sri Lanka. Even though a minority, the Christian faith has continued to impact the country significantly through governance, education, arts, social work and heritage. (Pinto: 2013)

The Anglican Church of Ceylon in Sri Lanka
The Church of England began in Sri Lanka in 1815. The Diocese of Colombo was founded in 1845. It was established by law in 1886. It then became a part of the Church of India Burma, Pakistan and Ceylon. With the division of this Province into united churches and the province of Myanmar, the two Dioceses of the Church of Ceylon, namely, the Diocese of Colombo and Diocese of Kurunagala, became what is known as "extra provincial Dioceses". The Diocese of Kurunagala was established in 1946 and was recognized legally in 1972.The Dioceses of Colombo and Kurunagala together, constitute the Church of Ceylon (Diocese of Colombo: 2015).

The Church of Ceylon today comprises over two hundred institutions including parishes, schools, children and old people's homes, farms, vocational training centres, social outreach centres and mission centres spread over each province and district in the country. From its inception the Church of Ceylon had to grapple with the multi-cultural situation in the country. Church membership is made up of Tamil, Sinhala and Burgher communities who speak English, Tamil and Sinhalese. It also boasts of varied and diverse socio-economic backgrounds ranging from the private schooled elite to the labourers and farmers of the country. Even today, almost 90% the Diocese of Kurunagala's membership is drawn from the plantation and village farmer communities. The first Bishop of the Diocese Rt Revd Lakdasa De Mel, confronted this reality with a holistic approach which proposed that this rich cultural mix must be made integral to the missional policy perspective of the Diocese. Thus, he reached into the arts, architecture, literature, customs, ideology and many other factors which were prevalent to adapt within the ministry of the Church. (Abayasekera: 2002)

The 1950's to the 1980's was a period of great change within the country. In one way it was the breaking away from the colonial past, but it also led to a vacuum which was to be filled up with indigenous resources, thinking, and potential. The Church was in a way influenced by these events and on top of that, the presence of a diverse cultural context required that the Church also had to adapt to be 'faithful in context' (Diocese of Kurunagala: 2019).

A Lesson from History in Contextualization
Roman Catholics, who had to practice their faith secretly under Dutch rule, pioneered indigenization. When the Dutch prohibited the Roman Catholic faith in Sri Lanka, most of the Dutch population was living in the coastal belt, where the Portuguese were once powerful. With prohibition, existence became difficult for Roman Catholics.

Those who were new to the Roman Catholic faith went back to Buddhism and Hinduism. Most of those who decided to remain Roman Catholic gradually migrated to the Kandyan kingdom, seeking the protection of the King of Kandy. This geographical move led these people reshape their faith in a new direction. In the new areas Roman Catholics had to survive without the government patronage which they had enjoyed for over one and a half centuries.

With the prohibition of Roman Catholicism, the Dutch expelled all priests from Sri Lanka. Roman Catholic believers in Sri Lanka survived for over thirty years without priests. Eventually, Father Joseph Vaz, a Brahmin Oratorian priest from India, came to Sri Lanka secretly and supported the faithful (Jose, 1996, 10). Later he was assisted by another Brahmin Oratorian priest, Jacome Gonsalves. These two priests promoted a more indigenous way of practising Christianity. They wrote books in Sri Lankan languages to promote the Catholic faith. In these books they were able to use Sri Lankan idioms to make their faith more meaningful to Roman Catholics. Considering these adaptations, the Dutch persecution of Roman Catholics was a blessing in disguise.

But the indigenization pioneered by Father Joseph Vaz came to an end at the beginning of the British era. With more religious freedom for Sri Lankan Roman Catholics more and more European priests came to Sri Lanka.

Under the British government it became important for Roman Catholics to be immersed in the English way of life, and so once again the Roman Catholic Church became more identified with the colonial power than with the ordinary people of Sri Lanka. This trend continued until the Second Vatican Council in the 1960's.

The Anglican Church and inculturation

Modern trends towards indigenization sprang up in the 19th century, in the Anglican Church and began to bear fruit in the early 20th century.

The classic example for this is the effort made at Baddegama in Galle, under the leadership of Lakdasa de Mel, who later became the Metropolitan Bishop in the Anglican Church for the Indian subcontinent. At Baddegama the use of the music of folk songs such as the boatmen's song, cartmen's song and the songs of the farmers became part of Christian worship. This process began in 1929 (Karunarathna: 2002). The importance of this musical setting for worship was that it was created when most Sri Lankan musicians held the view that all types of Sri Lankan music are from India. The importance of this musical setting is that it was done by Devar Suriya Sena even before the revival of Sinhala folk music by W.B. Makulloluwe.

Since the Christians of Moratuwa use Sinhala as their mother tongue these efforts of Devar Suriya Sena and Lakdasa de Mel became established in some Anglican churches in Moratuwa. Even today these Christians in

Moratuwa carry out this type of worship using folk music.

Attitudes to Local Cultures

The effects of this process of indigenization can be identified especially in the areas of Church architecture, customs, festivals, worship and music (Wickremasinghe: 2017, 27-28). In the area of Church architecture, efforts were made to change the Gothic style to Sri Lankan styles. Thus, in places such as Penideniya Training College, Trinity College Kandy, the Church of the Healing Christ in Kadalana, Moratuwa, and in the Cathedral of Kurunegala, churches were built with an indigenized architectural style, similar to the ordinance halls of the Sinhala court and the octagonal shape of the Temple of the Tooth in Kandy.

To complement this architecture indigenous decorations such as Sesath[1] were placed inside some churches in Sri Lanka. Instead of candles, oil lamps were introduced into churches. Sitting on the floor inside the church, the pews having been taken away, and removing one's shoes inside the church were some other efforts in this process of indigenization. The altar itself served as the audience of the King with the Sesath and spears on either side. Processions were also made including drums and the conch shell. Processions in Hindu and Buddhist cultures were of a similar nature and this was quite smoothly absorbed into the Christian culture.

Where Church music is concerned, traditionally the organ was used in all main churches following the pattern of Western churches. With indigenization, experiments were made in using traditional local musical instruments, such as the violin, sitar, tabla and esraj.[2] Local and folk tunes became the base in creating lyrics to be sung in churches where these efforts were being made. These efforts were able to bring local Christians closer to the feelings of the common people in Sri Lanka.

Through such Christian worship congregations were able to keep alive these tunes connected with their work. Today these tunes have become popular in Sri Lanka through musical groups such as the Gypsies in

Moratuwa. Among these songs one of the most popular songs is called "Waduweden divirakine", which means, "Carpentry keeps us alive." In this process it is apparent that it involves the new use of old elements of the culture. Earlier this music was used to praise Lord Buddha or local tribal gods such as Vishnu or Kataragama: now it was used to praise the Christian God.

In the new use of the old element the forms often varied. When Christians used the Sinhala language, in places the language form became used in a new way. For instance, the greeting of Sinhala Christians, "Jesu Pihitai", gave a new form to the word "pihitai" in the Sinhala language. The meaning of "pihitai" in Sinhala is something like "getting help", but in the new form it replaced the word "blessing" in the Western thought form. Therefore, among Christians "pihitai" is commonly used for blessings from God. In all these re-inventions the meaning presented to society was new, as the context in which they have been used was entirely different.

The following examples of such attempts can be given. In marriage customs there is a practice among Christians to give a meal of rice called "Adara Batha" (which means the love feast) on the day before the marriage. This comes from the agricultural feudal set-up in Sri Lanka. Here we see how this custom was diffused into the marriage rituals of Christians. Some Christian leaders took steps to actively encourage diffusion inside the Christian Church. The introduction of the chanting of Mangala Ashtaka (marriage blessings), with Christianized words being put to traditional tunes in the marriage service is anotherexample.

Attitudes to Religions and Ideologies
Organizations such as the Christian Workers' Fellowship even included reading scripture like Tripitakas (Buddhist scripture) from sister faiths in their services, especially in their May Day service to commemorate workers. The service took on a liberation focus with the style and text. The offertory includes the tools of labour and the labour of the hands.

This annual service continues to this day with the participation of many people who may not be part of the established Church and this signifies the mutually enriching dialogue that the Church continues to have with socialist ideologies.

The formation of the monastic order at Devasaranaramaya was another step in the dialogue of the Church with Religions and Ideologies. Sevaka Yohan Devananda initiated a discussion between Buddhist, Christian and Marxist ideologies. The following Affirmation of Faith is adapted from the 'New World Liturgy' Sevaka Yohan experimented with, in his time at Devasaranaramaya.

We acknowledge our responsibility for sin and evil, in the world, in our country, in our work places, in our homes and schools, in our temples and churches.

We acknowledge our want of faith, hope and love. We acknowledge our pride, vanity and self indulgence.

We acknowledge our selfishness and narrowness of spirit and our exploitation of others. We acknowledge our failures and omissions in the care and service of others. We acknowledge divisions among us, and failures and omission in corporate action for justice for the oppressed.

We need cleansing and forgiveness and humility of spirit. We need new life, true community and real joy. We need liberation, reconciliation and peace.

(Silence)

We seek to change our lives and to change the organization of society. In order to help build a new society and a new humanity, a new heaven and a new earth.

We seek a revolution of mind and spirit, a revolution in the structures of society, a revolution in the human relationships between leaders and people, administrators and workers, teachers and pupils, parents and children, priests and laity. We seek liberation of all those who are oppressed. We see to commit ourselves to the struggle for liberation. We seek a new order of love, justice and peace that all may care. We seek sharing of power and resources, of leadership and responsibility. We seek day by day to translate principles into practice as far as we can, alongside the people according to dharma (USPG, 2016).

The text dwells on 'suffering' from all the three ideologies mentioned above and it talks of alleviation of suffering also from the three respective perspectives. It was a liturgy in which many could participate affirming their faith but also learning from the other.

The use of a variety of religious idioms and the expression of it in liturgies that became contextualized developed after the independence of the country. The prayer book in 1970 in the Sinhala translation saw an attempt of using the local terminology to denote theological and ecclesiological concepts. One example of this is the 'Jaya Mangala Gatha' a Pali and then Sinhala poem of blessing of Buddhist origin which has got incorporated in Christianity. Another is the use of the flatbread 'roti' or 'chapathi' which has become the norm in communion services today. This has been influenced by other oriental religions and being the symbol of nourishment of the working masses it has embedded a liberation spirit into the service.

The practice of 'Thai Pongal', a festival of Tamil origin of new beginnings and thanking the Sun, has been in practice interpreted by many congregations in the Church as a harvest festival with praise for God's creation of the environment. The red sash shown symbolizing divinity which is wrapped around a coconut husk in Hinduism is replaced by a cross. Vesak, the Buddhist festival of the remembrance of the birth, enlightenment and demise of Lord Buddha, and the festival of Diwali are interpreted as 'Festivals of Lights' by Christians.

Another key moment in the Church's dialogue with religions and ideologies can be seen in the institution of the Theological College of Lanka, the only ecumenical seminary of the main-line Protestant churches in the country. In 1963 a decision was taken of building the college in Pilimatalawa. It was to be a 'Swabahsa' or local language college, in the language of instruction, in the worship and architecture of the chapel, and in the celebration of local festivals with a Christian interpretation. It was a significant step in the direction of the nationalism of the times, and in inculturation in worship, thought and study.

Worship is at the heart of this student community and takes place three times a day, morning, noon and evening, in Sinhala, Tamil and English. Aspects of monasticism have also been incorporated into this worship pattern with meditation practiced before each service. The chapel is decorated with Sri Lankan woodcarvings. The congregation removes their footwear and sit on the floor. Indigenous musical instruments mainly accompany worship. Guitars are used where appropriate, without displacing the indigenous atmosphere of worship. Mandatory courses on world religions are designed to make students aware of the multitude of ideologies, spiritualities and philosophies which aim to develop humanity in diverse ways.

The Continuing Dialogue

The Church of Sri Lanka is blessed to be surrounded by a host of living religions, ideologies and mysticisms. The Church is motivated towards contextualization in that in each locality different cultures exist side by side with Christianity. The Church also has an impetus from a nationalistic perspective in that it had to take on the role of being a local Church rather than a branch of an international western church after the independence of the country. It also had to come into an understanding of the numerous philosophies that came to be part of the national ideology, such as Marxism. The Church continues to be motivated by congregations who although being Christian belong to cultures and subcultures within the majority religions of the country. Such continuing dialogue, especially within Anglicanism, is a natural belonging rather than a forced attempt at relevance. In many ways the

Sri Lankan experience of being incarnated in context has much to offer in terms of contextualization and inculturation to the wider Church.

Endnotes

1. A type of fan as a symbol of represent authority and as a shade for the (Buddhist) priests, kings and the nobility. It was used as a decorative item and occasionally used for the earlier indented purposes too, at ceremonial functions weddings and even at funerals.

2. Dilruba and esraj have combined characteristics of the sitar and sarangi. These have long necks, frets and metal strings of the sitar, but unlike the sitar, they have a sound box with parched skin and are played by bow like the sarangi.

3

The Ceylon Liturgy

Phillip Tovey

Anglican missionaries included the translation of the Bible and the Book of Common Prayer as a part of their core activity. A prayer book (without ordinal and articles) was published in Sinhala in 1820, and various other editions were later produced, Griffiths (2001) includes 12 different editions up to1955. The first Tamil translation is from 1802 and various later editions, Griffiths includes 27, but some are produced for South India. This practice shows a translation model of inculturation (Tovey, 2004, 4). This, however, was gradually challenged and adaptations to local culture began in various ways.

The work of the Oxford Movement stimulated liturgical reform internationally, both with catholic mission societies promoting more catholic worship in some dioceses and with more independent evangelical churches such as the Free Church of England and the Reformed Episcopal Church producing more evangelical liturgy. In Ceylon there were both low church CMS missionaries and higher church SPG missionaries and so the diocese had a mixture of approaches.

The 1928 Prayer Book in England was a part of a world-wide movement of liturgical change which also influenced Ceylon. It is often said that the agents of inculturation were the missionaries, but this was not so in Sri Lanka. In 1927 Rev G.S. Amarasekara, senior priest of the diocese, petitioned the bishop Mark Carpenter-Garnier (an Englishman) on behalf of the Ceylonese clergy for a diocesan liturgy. A committee was set up to produce a liturgy, the first draft coming in 1931. This version was referred to the Consultative Body of the Lambeth Conference, who sent it to Bishop Frere and Chancellor Srawley. This was given sanction for experimental use in 1933 by the Episcopal Synod. In 1938 it was authorised for Alternative use by the Provincial Synod. In the various iterations of the text Ceylonese clergy and laity took a full part in the decision making at Synod and committee stages. This was something locally produced but with international conversation. It was described by Beven (1946, 117) as:

> an attempt … to give the religious consciousness of the people of the land an opportunity of adequate expression.

It was one of the first liturgies of the Anglican communion to systematically attempt do this.

The First Draft

The initial text was published in 1931 and called *An Order for the Administration of the Holy Communion* (Ceylon Liturgy Committee, 1931) The document has text on one page and notes on the other as to sources and documents that have influenced the text. The curators of the liturgy were aware of liturgical revision in other parts of the communion quoting England 1549 and 1928, South Africa, the USA, Scotland, and the Bombay liturgy. There is also an awareness of eastern liturgies, articles written by Brightman, and books from the Alcuin Club.

One source of particular interest is John Blomfield (1930), *The Eucharistic Canon*. Blomfield was an Australian liturgist, not currently well known, who wrote an important book for the time on eucharistic liturgy. He saw the anaphora as comprising of three sections, thanksgiving, offering and invocation. He was particularly influenced by classical anaphoras from the east and spends considerable time discussing the epiclesis. He has no problem with a consecratory epiclesis after the narrative of institution, which caused problems in South Africa (Hinchliff, 1959).

There were various changes on the way to the approved text. This table gives some indication of the differences.

The 1931 Order	The 1933 Liturgy
The Introduction	*The Introduction*
Hymn / Psalm / introit	Hymn
	Collect for purity
	Confession
	Kyrie
Gloria	Gloria
Collect	Collect
The Ministry of the Word	*The Ministry of the Word*
Epistle	Epistle
Psalm / Hymn	Psalm / Hymn
Gospel	Gospel
	Creed
Sermon	Sermon
Creed	
The Offertory	*The Offertory*
Sentences	Sentences
Preparation of the table	Preparation of the table
Alms	Alms
Prayer for Church Militant (modified)	Litany
The Consecration	*The Consecration*
Eucharistic Prayer	Eucharistic Prayer
	Lord's Prayer
	The Peace
	Benedictus

The 1931 Order	The 1933 Liturgy
The Communion	*The Communion*
Lord's Prayer	
Fraction	
Commixture	
Benedictus	
The Peace	
	Humble Access
Agnus Dei	Agnus Dei
Invitation	Invitation
Communion	Communion
The Thanksgiving	*The Thanksgiving*
Prayer of Thanksgiving	Prayer of Thanksgiving
Blessing (2 forms)	Blessing

This chart enables us to see that there were key structural changes in the introduction, with elements from a preparatory service been transferred into the main service in the later text. There was also considerable reordering after the eucharistic prayer and the loss of a separate fraction and commixture.

Jasper (1954, 252-255) comments on the response to English consultation was that many of the suggestions were incorporated, but not all: there was no alternative use of the beatitudes or alternative consecration prayers. In 1933 a note in Theology by WK Lowther Clarke on the 1932 approved text described the rite as 'very beautiful and workmanlike and repays careful study' (101).

Structure of the Approved Text

The service was adapted in light of the comments made and was locally approved in 1933 (Wigan, 1964). It was very different to the 1662 Holy Communion that was being used in Ceylon at the time. The table below gives the structure of the liturgy.

The Introduction
Hymn
Collect for purity
Confession
Kyrie
Gloria
Collect
The Ministry of the Word
Epistle
Psalm / Hymn
Gospel
Creed
Sermon
The Offertory
Sentences
Preparation of the table
Alms
Litany
The Consecration
Eucharistic Prayer
Lord's Prayer
The Peace
Benedictus
The Communion
Humble Access
Agnus Dei
Invitation
Communion
The Thanksgiv ing
Prayer of Thanksgiving
Blessing

There are general rubrics, a pre-communion devotion, a form for supplementary consecration, additional sentences and a selection of proper prefaces. The service is written assuming that a deacon will be present and taking a full part.

To modern eyes this structure is not remarkable, but in 1933 this was revolutionary. The order of the service by Cranmer in 1552 was reversed to more of a 1549 classical pattern. The absence of an Old Testament lesson reflects its vintage and the peace looks, for many Anglicans today, an odd position. The offertory is in a prayer book position (in the middle of the service rather than before the eucharistic prayer). The intercessions in the form of a litany are also in the prayer book position.

The eucharistic prayer is distinctive. The structure is that of traditional anaphora, incorporating prayer book manual acts, but an eastern epiclesis. The text is a careful weaving together of prayer book tradition and the Liturgy of St James. The only other liturgy of the time to make such a move was the 1920 Bombay liturgy. This was curated as a 'plea for a distinctive liturgy for the Indian Church' (texts at Wohlers). There are many differences between these two liturgies, the Bombay liturgy following much closer the Liturgy of St James. Perhaps the context of each is significant, the Bombay liturgy being written for an ashram and the Ceylon Liturgy for parish use. So, within the liturgical renewal of the 1920s and 30s Ceylon had taken a distinctive eastward turn compared to the western models that were developed in other Provinces. This is in part due to the local tradition of the visit of St Thomas to Sri Lanka, historical evidence of Eastern Christians in Ceylon and the presence of the Orthodox Churches in the neighbouring Travancore and Cochin, present day Kerala.

The communion rite is a version of a more catholic Anglican tradition. The thanksgiving is traditionally Anglican as is the blessing. The order for a second consecration follows 1662 in its existence but adds the epiclesis as an essential element.

The elements of the service in more detail

In the introduction the confession does not follow the 1662 wording, unlike most of the revisions of the day. The Gloria is allowed at this point or later and in two different forms.

The priest says the sentences while the alms are collected. These are a variety of Biblical texts, including additional texts for feast days. Some of these texts might be interpreted as relating to eucharistic offering, of some sort, but this is not entirely clear. The intercessions (a new litany with some elements from 1662) are led by the deacon.

The Consecration, (eucharistic prayer but not called such), begins in the normal way with a threefold dialogue, going back to patristic precedent. The preface follows Anglican patterns with a short paragraph and then a variety of proper prefaces, in this case a richer collection than the 1662 prayer book. The pre-sanctus and sanctus are Anglican. The next two paragraphs are from the Liturgy of St James. The first picks up on the word holy and leads adoration of each of the persons of the Trinity, acknowledging their holiness. The next paragraph follows St James in rehearsing the economy of salvation, the marring of the image of God and the loving response of various prophets leading to the coming of the Son of God to renew the image. A familiar paragraph from Anglican sources is included to talk of the perfection of the work of the cross. The Narrative of Institution includes the manual acts (there is no later fraction). The language of the narrative is an incorporation of elements of St James into the Anglican pattern:

> He took (Bread, the Cup)
> When he had given thanks to thee…
> He blessed it…

The additional emphasis is on the blessing of the Bread and Cup. This comes from the Matthew – Mark tradition where blessed is used instead of giving thanks. Here in the Ceylon liturgy both exist. In St James the emphasis is on 'He blessed' and the force of the wording suggest that this was not just a historical reference. Lowther Clarke commented:

Probably ευλογησας and ευχαριστησαςas in the Gospels are identical in meaning, but the fact that giving thanks *was* the way of blessing food requires two words in English, if it is to be understood. (Lowther Clarke, 1933, 102)

It would appear that later, this was not understood.

The anamnesis follows the wording of the 1928 prayer book but adding his seating in heaven and his coming again.

Having in remembrance the precious death and passion of thy dear Son, his mighty resurrection, his ascension into heaven, and his session in glory, and looking for his coming again;

This is a more eastern emphasis and celebrates the whole economy of salvation looking for its completion.

There is a mild oblation which follows on directly from the anamnesis:

According to his holy institution, do celebrate, and set forth before thy Divine Majesty with these gifts, the memorial which he hath commanded us to make

This is entirely from 1928.

The epiclesis asks the Spirit to be sent upon us and these gifts. This is a reworking of the 1928 wording, with a different emphasis but little significant difference.

And we beseech thee most merciful Father to hear us and to send thy Holy Spirit upon us and upon these thy gifts, that they, being blessed and hallowed by his lifegiving power, may be unto us the Body and

Blood of thy most dearly beloved Son, to the end that we, receiving the same, may be sanctified both in body and soul, and preserved unto life everlasting.

While both Jasper (1989) and Kennedy (2008) look at Scotland as the major influence of the epiclesis, it is by no means a copying of the Scottish 1928 epiclesis. The first draft had a simpler epiclesis. It was also aware of criticism of the epiclesis in *Theology* 1927 which made a categorical distinction of invocation on persons and things. This question is to be returned to in later revision, but the emphasis in the more eastern epiclesis is to see both persons and things as both God's creatures, both being redeemed by the work of the Son of God culminating in the cross and resurrection, both needing renewal by the Spirit.

The rest of the prayer is from the 1928 alternative prayer of consecration, which itself is a reworking and reordering of the Prayer Book.

The rest of the service continues with standard Anglican elements. The words of administration are worth noting:

> The Body of Christ, the bread of life
> The blood of Christ, the chalice of life.

The rubric continues to require any remaining elements to be consumed.

This analysis of the text might suggest some adaptation to context, but the story of this liturgy is not only about liturgical text but music and architecture. This is a much more far reaching contextualisation than appears on paper.

Musical settings
Worship is not just about liturgical text; the context and setting can be equally important. Lakdasa DeMel commented that it was not enough to produce Ceylonese Christians, they had to be Christian Ceylonese.

The aspect of foreignness had to go and be replaced by an authentic Ceylonese Christianity. Music was one of the areas discussed:

> Both in Sinhalese and Tamil there are certain set forms of verse traditional to our literature. The music of the Tamils has had a great tradition in singing divine praises in the Hindu Temple and elsewhere. The compositions of the learned musician who performed chamber music at Court are also available, but too elaborate generally speaking, for congregational worship as we need it in Church. There remains the great body of living folk music which when carefully studied and purged of frivolity is just what we need. (DeMel, 1955, 38)

Lakdasa DeMel was deeply involved in fostering musical development.

The Sinhalese setting of the liturgy was published in 1941 *A Sinhalese Setting of the Ceylon Liturgy*. This was composed by Devar Surya Sena, who was to become a noted Sri Lankan musicologist and composer. He collected folk tunes and then set and adapted them for the liturgy. It was first sung in Baddegama in 1932 and with the encouragement of the vicar, his cousin Lakdasa de Mel became the setting for that church. The aim was to provide a 'Sinhalese musical setting' and not an adapted western musical version. Local instruments were encouraged, and the use of organ and western instruments discouraged. Once again this was a radical step in the inter-war period. Similar work was done to produce a Tamil setting by Mr and Mrs Anandanayagam (Markham, 2013, 365)

Devar Surya Sena (1954) wrote more about the setting in the *Centenary Book*. He laments the use of western instruments and translated hymns in many services in Ceylon. This he sees as giving some evidence that Christianity is a 'denationalising force'. He notes increasing music round the world sung to local tunes. While recognising the need for musical expertise, with which he was well supplied, he applauds various attempts at inculturation and commends the setting he composed. He notes the key place played in this development by Lakdasa de Mel.

The Sunday Times (2015), quoted him on the liturgy saying:

> The majestic theme of the Gajaga Vannama seemed to fit the Sanctus; a suggestion of the Boatman's Song – Sivpada tune seemed just right for the Agnus Dei. Bit by bit themes for each part of the service up to the Gloria were given to me. I was merely a channel. Some unseen power seemed to be directing.

Architecture and art

Lakdasa DeMel (1955, 2) was also interested in the architectural context of worship.

The most obvious witness to the Church being indigenous is the employment of the national architecture. He notes the chapel in Trinity College Kandy (built 1935), the Teacher Training Institution in Peradeniya (built 1920) and Kurunagala Cathedral (built 1960).

Sagara Jayasinghe (2015, 2) shows how these churches were part of a wider movement which he calls the 'decolonization process of religious architecture'. Trinity College chapel is perhaps a good place to start. The similarity with the king's Audience Hall in the Temple of the Tooth in Kandy is striking. A series of stone pillars with a podium at one end, with no walls and capitals of the pillars with traditional designs, describes both buildings. This was a radical step away from the Victorian gothic of other churches. The chapel also includes life size murals on the walls.

In 1928 Lakdasa DeMel was made superintendent missionary of Baddegama. The church had been built in 1824 and was now in a very poor state. The new priest put much energy into rebuilding.

> Reinforced concrete pillars of Kandyan design replaced the old wooden pillars. The communion rails and raredos were decorated in the ancient "Sittara" style. The worshippers using the Ceylon Liturgy... (Christ Church, 2019)

The new priest also encouraged the wearing of local dress and removed many of the pews to allow sitting on the floor.

The furnishings of the sanctuary were completely renewed. The cross on the altar was that of the Anuradhapura Cross (Somaratna, 1996). Similar ancient "Persian" crosses are found in Kerala (Vazhuthanapally, 1988). This cross is used almost universally in the Church of Ceylon. Around the altar stand local lamps of brass that can used coconut oil, rather than candles. There are two standing censers at the alter which use incense on sticks. On the pillars rest two fans of circular local design (in some churches these are accompanied by spears). This arrangement has become very common in Sri Lankan churches and totally reflects local culture.

Art was also a part of the 'indigenisation' of mission (Karunaratne, 2002).

> The reredos and altar rails were painted with Kandyan art forms the like of which can be seen in the cultural centres of worship in Kandy and Kelaniya.

Much of this he paid for himself. This movement of local art being incorporated into churches has continued to today. Elizabeth Harris (2016) reviews the whole movement and sees it as a Christian rapprochement with Buddhism. The movement has not been systematically examined but this was considerably improved by a recent publication by the National Christian Council of Sri Lanka (2014), which brings together many examples of this movement.

Thus art, architecture, furnishings, dress and music were all addressed in the creation of the Ceylon Liturgy in what we might now call the inculturation of Christian worship. This was developed and furthered by Sri Lankan Christians.

Later revisions

After 50 years of use there were some people who wanted a revision of the liturgy. Some changes of a rubrical nature were made in 1977 but more radical changes were made in, 1987, 1988 and 2013. Some of the changes were of a positive nature, the use of modern English, the addition of an Old Testament lesson, the moving of the peace to before the offertory, the increase of congregational participation. All of these were a positive development updating the liturgy to the 'norms' of the contemporary Liturgical Movement. The eucharistic prayer was also reworked, but not so skilfully.

Narmmasena Wickremasinghe (2011, 90-91) indicates that the push for change was from an evangelical group who wanted to withdraw all words 'inconsistent with the pure word of God'. There was no change up to the sanctus. In the post sanctus 'sages' were added to the list of God's guidance, formerly only 'the law and the prophets'. More congregational responses were added to the text. Surprisingly the prayer book wording about the cross was removed and replaced with a congregational response:

Father, Jesus loved us
And sacrificed himself for us… (1987, 1988, 2013 -modified)

A rather more anodyne description of the crucifixion. The Narrative of Institution was recast in the Luke-Pauline tradition avoiding the Biblical words 'he blessed'.

The anamnesis is recast. The Ceylon Liturgy said:

Having in remembrance the precious death and passion of thy dear Son, his mighty resurrection, his ascension into heaven, and his session in glory, and looking for his coming again

This is recast to:

> We celebrate your Son's death and victory, giving thanks for all he has done for us (1987, 1988, 2013).

This redaction limits the focus of the economy of salvation and potentially cuts the eucharist from the Ascension and Parousia.

The epiclesis seems to be particularly difficult. The Ceylon Liturgy said:

> And we beseech thee, most merciful Father, to hear us, and to send thy Holy Spirit upon us and upon these thy gifts, that they, being blessed and hallowed by his life-giving power, may be unto us the Body and Blood of thy most dearly beloved Son, to the end that we, receiving the same, may be sanctified both in body and soul, and preserved unto life everlasting.

The 1987 version said:

> We entreat you Most Merciful Father that your Holy Spirit may hallow the whole earth and us, as we partake in the body and blood of your dearly loved Son, and unite us with all creation.

The 1988 version said:

> We entreat you Most Merciful Father that your Holy Spirit may hallow us, (and these your gifts by his life-giving power, that they may be for us the Body and Blood of your most dearly loved Son).

It is very unusual to have a section in brackets in an authorised liturgy at such a crucial point, the implication that one can leave out that section if desired (Kennedy, 2008).

The 2013 liturgy has two alternative epicleses:

And we entreat you, most merciful Father, to hear us, and send your All Holy Spirit upon + us and upon these your gifts, that they being blessed and hallowed by that life-giving power, may be for us the Body and Blood of your most dearly loved Son, to the end that we receiving the same may be sanctified and filled with your grace and heavenly blessing.

This is a return to a the more traditional epiclesis undoing the revisions of the 1980s. The alternative is:

And we entreat you, most merciful Father that your Holy Spirit may hallow the whole earth and us, as we partake in the body and blood of your dearly loved Son, and unite us with your new creation that we receiving the same may be sanctified and filled with your grace and heavenly blessing.

It is not clear why there is a change in capitalisation of Body and Blood. This alternative has stronger creation-new creation themes.

The anamnetic and epicleptic parts of the revisions somewhat reduce the theology of the rites and it not clear that the move expresses the 'clear word of God' anymore that the 1933 version. However, Bishop Jabez Gnanapragasam commented that the intention of the compliers was to provide and original and authentic liturgy for today's Sri Lanka (Chapman, 2015). There are clear advances in congregational participation and the Ministry of the Word.

Conclusion
This brief history of the Ceylon Liturgy shows that questions of inculturation go back to the 1930s in Sri Lanka. This was a movement of local people and changes were made not just to liturgical text but

the whole setting of the liturgy, in the building, furnishings, art forms and song. It is this thorough contextualisation that makes the Ceylon Liturgy so interesting, and a pioneer in Anglicanism. However, we see that 50 years later questions of contextualization still appear, the new has become the old, and further work is required for the context of the day.

4

Alternative Contextualization: The New World Liturgy and The Workers' Mass

Marc Billimoria

Introduction

The Sri Lankan church historian G. P. V. Somaratna has recognized that unlike the Roman Catholic missionaries during the Portuguese period, later Dutch and British missionaries did not use available 'bridges' to share and proclaim the Gospel in a culture influenced richly by Buddhism and Hinduism (Somaratna 2006: 4 - 5). Indigenization was generally regarded with suspicion for fear of syncretism. The perceived foreignness of the Gospel led historians like K. M. De Silva to conclude:

> Christianity was interpreted on western lines, and in non-indigenous concepts. The missionaries imposed on their adherents in Sri Lanka the conventional forms of Western Christianity almost in their entirety, oblivious of the value of indigenous art forms – music, drumming, dance and architecture – to Christian worship.
> (De Silva 1978: 221)

The cultural renaissance and the movement for independence from colonial rule that emerged in the late 19th century forced churches to re-examine their methods for more effective and relevant mission.

Anglican Initiatives

During the early decades of the 20th century, responding to the nationalistic spirit of the age, Anglicans began to engage seriously with indigenization at many levels (Chapman, Clarke & Percy 2016: 224). The *Ceylon Liturgy* (1938) for example, was a catalyst for indigenization of liturgical space, vesture, gesture and posture with more changes than the 1662 Book of Common Prayer had ever allowed before (Martin and Mullen 1981: 6). An early pioneer of the movement, Bishop Lakdasa de Mel, justified the need for change in *The Christian Liturgy in Ceylon* (Seabury-Western Theological Seminary, 1956). As Bishop Duleep de Chickera, among others, has shown during that the fifty years since the *Ceylon Liturgy* Anglican worship in Sri Lanka has been transformed (Markham, Hawkins IV, Terry, and Steffenson 2013: 365). By 1988 and the first full revision of the *Ceylon Liturgy* (Evans and Wright: 1991, 587 – 588), lay theologians and liturgical scholars who had been heavily influenced and inspired by a radical spirit of the age ensured a liturgy in which there was dynamic interaction between the Gospel and the cultural context. Significantly it was during this period, in 1972, that terminology changed, and indigenization evolved into contextualization (Fabella and Sugirtharajah 2003: 58).

Yet while *A Liturgy for Sri Lanka* (1988), was 'radical', it was not as 'revolutionary' as two attempts at liturgical experimentation rooted in the fermenting socio-political context of post-independence Sri Lanka in the 1950s and 1960s. David J. Kennedy, has recognized that attempts to indigenize the official liturgies of the Church of Ceylon were limited in scope, too traditional and conservative, and has identified the *Workers' Mass* of the Christian Workers' Fellowship (1968) and the *New World Liturgy* of the Devasaranaramaya (1973) as fuller examples of contextualization (Kennedy 2016: 214), though they are not strictly Anglican but ecumenical, and would be better referred to as examples of 'alternative contextualization'.

The New World Liturgy (NWL)

In 1957, three years after his ordination, the Oxbridge educated Anglican priest John Cooray, who had already by this time changed his name to Yohan Devananda and adopted indigenous clothing, founded Devasaranaramaya (Ashram of Divine Refuge), an Anglican monastic community in a rural parish of the Diocese of Kurunegala with the blessings of Bishop Lakdasa de Mel. That this took place in the wake of the socio-political revolution of 1956, barely ten years after independence from colonial rule, was no coincidence. Devasaranaramaya, like other Christian Ashrams of the time, drew inspiration from both the Hindu *Asrama* and Buddhist *Aramaya* traditions. Devananda combined contemplative spirituality with a programme of ecumenical dialogue, and social activism (Dan O'Connor, Church Times, 15th July 2016) in a 'Living Dialogue' drawing in not just Christians but also people of other faiths and ideologies. There emerged a movement for human liberation that sought to address the burning issues being faced by rural peasants, youth, workers, students and other marginalized communities. For example, during the Marxist youth insurgency of 1971 Devananda began a collective farm at Devasaranaramaya at the request of unemployed youth and with the blessings of Bishop Lakshman Wickremesinghe of Kurunegala. Devananda, whose radicalism was not acknowledged by the Church establishment (William L. Sachs 2018: 89 – 91), operated on the margins of Church life and was often critical of comfortable Christianity. Nurtured in the Anglo-Catholic liturgical tradition and influenced by Gabriel Hebert's *Liturgy & Society* Movement, Devananda's activism was undergirded by sacramental spirituality and thus Devasaranaramaya soon also became a centre for bold contextual liturgical innovation and experimentation that

> became an outstanding model for combining meditation and action, withdrawal and engagement, contemplation and struggle. (Ariarajah 2018: 80)

Writing in 1975, Devananda outlined the development of Devasaranaramaya's liturgical life and his rationale for the NWL described as 'a para-liturgical form':

> created to enable full participation by people of all religions and ideologies (1973). The common theme or concern is the movement for development, justice and liberation – its joys and struggles – its heights and depths. (Diocese of Kurunegala: 1975)

He saw the NWL and the other liturgies produced for the Community as the result of

> the articulation and crystallization of years of living dialogue... an attempt to integrate the values of the past with the values of the new world...(DOK: 1975)

Ulrich Dornberg in his study of contextual theology and social change in Sri Lanka views Devananda's hermeneutical stance of the mutual engagement between 'self-criticism' and 'social change' as the basis of the NWL in which there is both "conversion and revolution", where theology is

> an expression of the search for authenticity, for integration of religion with life, meditation with action, peace with justice. (Dornberg: 147)

A closer look at the text of the NWL will illustrate this dialectic.

The Order of Service (1973/1979 Version)	Commentary
The Truth Overcome (Preparation)	Seek the truth **Listen to the truth** Love the truth **Serve the truth** Teach the truth **Live the truth** Defend the truth **Unto death**
Silence	The first of many periods of silence
Giving Honour	Respectful homage is paid to the Hindu sages, the Buddha, the Lord Jesus Christ, the Prophet Mohammed, Karl Marx, all creative artists and scientists, all wise statesmen and leaders, all saints and martyrs, sages and prophets, ordinary people, workers and peasants, teachers and students, parents and children.
Silence Awareness	This is a section in the Liturgy which is akin to a penitential rite where an awareness of self is the focus.
Silence Seeking	A section during which the worshipper focuses on change and transformation and a commitment to the struggle for liberation.
Silence Dialogue	This section is basically the Ministry of the Word that includes readings from the ancient religions, modern ideologies and any other relevant writings, preaching of a sermon, or dialogue and discussion, self-criticism and mutual criticism.
The Preparation of the Gifts	In contextual form

37

The Order of Service (1973/1979 Version)	Commentary
The Celebration and Sharing of Food	This is basically the Great Thanksgiving of this Liturgy but includes quotations from the Upanishads, the Buddha, Jesus Christ, the Prophet Mohammed, Karl Marx, Che Guevara and Mao Tse Tung. While food and drink are passed around from hand to hand (Communion) individuals explain the meaning of the common action using their own words or the text provided in the liturgy itself.
Conclusion	The Liturgy ends with the singing of a hymn or lyric, the National Anthem or the Internationale before which representatives of the workers, peasants, students and other groups present will receive the symbols of their work to carry out in the recessional. The final words of the Liturgy are *OM SHANTI (a Hindu term meaning 'peace for all creation') SHALOM VIMUKTI (a term meaning 'liberty' or 'liberation')*

While the words of the Rite are the main focus there are very few rubrics concerning ceremonial acts, gesture or posture. There is only a note relating to the periods of silence and the start of different sections of the Liturgy that are signalled by the ringing of a small bell (1973: 12). There are no directions for clergy as the focus is on a celebration by the entire community thus the Leader could well be a lay person, all pointing to the radical nature of the NWL.

Inspiration for the NWL also came from Devananda's involvement with the Christian Workers' Fellowship (CWF) and the *creative liturgical interaction* that existed between the CWF and Devasaranaramya (Jeffrey and Annathaie Abayasekera, 2016).

The Workers' Mass (WM)

The mission of the Christian Workers' Fellowship, founded in 1958 by Vijaya Vidyasagara and other like-minded Christian Socialists, is rooted in liturgical spirituality. At the heart of its activities is the so-called *Workers' Mass* that on May Day is attended by members and supporters of the CWF before they join their respective trade union or party rallies in the afternoon.

The rationale for the CWF was influenced by the writings of Anglican thinkers such as F. D. Maurice, Charles Gore, Henry Scott Holland, Matthew Headlam, Conrad Noel, William Temple, and John Robinson, as well as the social teachings of the Fathers of the Early Church.

The theology of the CWF has also been enriched by both Buddhist and Hindu philosophy as well as Marxist ideology and the WM as well as other CWF liturgies reflect the socio-cultural, political and religious context of Sri Lanka.

Addressing the 122nd session of the Diocesan Council of the Anglican Diocese of Colombo in 2007, Vidyasagara, considered a modern-day prophet by many, articulated the vision of the CWF vis a vis the WM:

The naturalness with which people of other faiths and persuasions are able to participate in CWF services is itself confirmation of the power of Christ to draw and unite people when he is presented in a manner intelligible to their cultural ethos and thought forms... In the Workers' Mass for instance there is found a truly Asian harmony of word and silence, of stillness and movement. The ceremonial of the Mass too is essentially local in character. The national dress of the servers, the use of sesath, pandams and incense burners of the type used in temple processions, the dancing during offertory, the prostration after the elevation, the manual gestures of the clergy and people together with the musical orchestration and the blowing of the conch shell and sounding of drums all contribute to making this liturgy a truly Sri Lankan product. It is the CWF's conviction that the

Mass as the symbol and foretaste of God's Kingdom, the new classless society of the future, must be celebrated with the utmost beauty of colour and movement, of sound and scent, and reflect all that is best in our culture (Revelation 20: 26).

The Mass ends with the singing of the Sri Lankan version of the Internationale, thus underlying the connection between the Mass and the struggle of the masses for liberation. (Vidyasagara 2007: 5 – 6)

Ulrich Dornberg has identified two significant aspects that define the liturgy's radical theology, that he calls 'Kingdom of God theology', namely that the Reign of God transcends the Church and secondly that the Reign of God was inaugurated by the incarnation of Christ (Dornberg 1991: 135). Thus, given CWF's self-understanding of itself as a defiantly political movement both transcending and staying within the Church, its members believe that the Holy Eucharist should be open to all, including non-Christians (*For a Real Sri Lankan Church*, Colombo CWF: 1984).

The WM as we have it today was first used in 1968 and revised for the 6th time in 1991/1992, crafted entirely by lay people led by Vidyasagara, many of whom were not even Christian themselves, such as Premaranjith Tilakeratne and Austin Munasinghe, local musicians and dramatists who were both Buddhists (Workers' Mass Liturgy, Christian Workers' Fellowship 1968, 6th revision 1991/1992, Reprint May Day 1993).

The Structure of the WM is closer to the traditional Anglican Eucharist than the NWL. The footnotes give further examples from the text.

Order of service (1991/1992 Revised Version)	Commentary
Procession	Litany 28 stanzas Chanted to the tune of a Pilgrim Chant used by devotees climbing Adam's Peak

Order of service (1991/1992 Revised Version)	Commentary

The Preparation
  Lamp lighting
  Gloria or Magnificat
  Penitential rite
  Absolution
	The Lamp symbolizing the presence of God is lit accompanied by the blowing of the Conch shell, the beating of drums, incense and fire
	
	Various alternatives are provided including one in English from the special Eucharistic Liturgy of St. Mark's-in-the-Bouwerie, New York

Ministry of Word
  Introductory text
  Contemporary reading
  OT or NT
  Little entrance
  Gospel
 	
  Sermon
 	
  Song of threefold refuge
	From Upanishads[4]
	From other religious texts or ideological texts
	
	The Gospel Procession
	On May Day it is always Matthew 25: 31 – 46 either read or chanted by one person or dramatized by a group of persons
	Through dialogue or drama, the reading of a statement or traditional homily
	The Thisaranaya, a credal response and affirmation of refuge in the Holy Trinity

Intercessions Collect	Always the Collect by Archbishop William Temple[5]

The Ministry of the Sacrament
  Sharing of peace
 	
  Great entrance
	[6]Accompanied by the lighting of fire and the kindling of incense. The traditional greeting with palms together and a slight bow to one another, a hand clasp, mutual embrace or kiss of peace follows
	The Red Flag, implements and tools of the workers and the elements of bread, water and wine as well as offerings of flowers, light (fire), dance, sounds (bells and drums) and scent (incense) are offered up during the Offertory Hymn

Order of service (1991/1992 Revised Version)	Commentary

The Ministry of the Sacrament (continued)
   Offertory chant
 	
   The Great Thanksgiving
	The four elements of earth, water, fire and air are offered back to the Creator while water is sprinkled on the oblations, the altar is censed, and homage given to it with Agni
	Three options

The Communion Lord's Prayer Commixture Elevation Prostration Communion	The four elements of earth, water, fire and air are offered back to the Creator while water is sprinkled on the oblations, the altar is censed, and homage given to it with Agni Deep Silence & Prostration by the clergy and others who have concelebrated All present, Christian and non-Christian, are invited to share
	Return of the Red Flag and symbols of labour.[7] Singing the Internationale

The use of silence throughout the service is a reflection of the influence of Asian spirituality while the deep prostration by the clergy and people following the Elevation is a local practice that has been adopted even in mainstream Anglican liturgical practice.

The red vestments worn by the clergy with the white hammer and sickle motif emblazoned on them and the offering up of various symbols of labour together with the elements during the Great Entrance have been influenced by Conrad Noel's Thaxted Movement as is the singing of the Internationale with which the liturgy ends when clergy and people following a large red flag march out of the worship space with clenched fists raised to start the 'Liturgy after the Liturgy'.

Eastern and Oriental Orthodox influence can be seen in the Little Entrance (Gospel Procession) and the Great Entrance (Offertory Procession), the Epiclesis (invocation of the Holy Spirit over the gifts) in the Eucharistic prayer where it is placed after the Anamnesis (memorial of the acts of redemption) rather than before as in the western usage, and the solemn Elevation immediately before Communion with the proclamation 'The gifts of God, for the People of God.'

Non-Christian influences include the use of readings from sacred scriptures of one of the other religions of the country such as the *Tripitaka* of the Buddhists, the Upanishads of the Hindus and the Qu'ran of the Muslims. Readings may also be taken from secular sources including the writings of Karl Marx, Che Guevera, Dom Helder Camera, or Desmond Tutu.

The new Eucharistic Prayer for the Liturgy introduced in 1994 saw the inclusion of terms such as Taraka (suggested by the renowned Jesuit scholar Fr Aloysius Peiris) which, as the note states, is a term used in Indic cultures to refer to:

One who not only crosses over to the further shore (from suffering to freedom) but also makes others cross over i.e., Liberator – Saviour – Soter. In Kalidasa's epic 'Kumarasambhava' (birth of the Saviour child) the child is called Taraka, the one who guides us through the ocean of samsara. (Eucharistic Prayer, Christian Workers' Fellowship, 1994)

On the whole the WM is a fine example of alternative contextualization. In the final analysis as Narmmasena Wickremesinghe points out,

The Workers' Mass… brings together both rural and urban Christian lay persons and Christian clergy from different denominational traditions. The very being of the worshipper is brought into the heart of the liturgy. It surpasses the barriers of ethnic, class and church divisions and brings to focus the lasting, just peace of human solidarity. It becomes indeed the Sacrament of Unity, the Sacrament of Worker Solidarity, and the Sacrament of Toiling Humanity. It is at once the 4000 year old national culture, the 2000 year old Christian culture, and the modern universal worker culture. It is indeed the original gospel in today's Sri Lanka. (Holeton (ed.) 1990: 54)

Conclusion

While the two examples of alternative contextualization examined have been groundbreaking, they have not been free of criticism.

The NWL is still used, but only within the confines of the Devasarana community. While its basic premise is a focus on community, fellowship and a new world order, the Church of Ceylon is yet to accept it. The WM is similarly only used at CWF events, although it has influenced the Sinhala translation of the 1988 Anglican revision and subsequent revisions of same. Many of the chants and parts of the Eucharistic Prayer of the 1988 *A Liturgy for Sri Lanka* are directly from the WM, though even some of these have been rejected by conservative Anglicans, who tend to omit them.

Critics of both the NWL and the WM point to what they view as the syncretism that is encouraged by the use of terminology, prayers, words, phrases and readings from non-Christian faiths and ideologies. They echo the words of liturgical scholars such as George Mathew,

> The use of indigenous sacred literature and theological concepts in the liturgy of the Church should be approached with proper caution. The inculturation process must be judged by its motives: does the use of the scriptures and theological concepts of other religions help the mission of the Church? So if inculturation leads to syncretism, such attempts should be discouraged. (Stevenson & Spinks, Mowbray: 1991, 153)

Contextualization, if too extreme works against the purpose for which it exists if it alienates worshipping communities. All attempts at contextualization therefore need to be mission oriented. As David Holeton has warned contextualization cannot be limited to one aspect only it must

> affect the whole ethos of corporate worship...The liturgy rightly constructed, forms the people of God, enabling and equipping them for their mission of evangelism and social justice in their culture and society. (Holeton, 1989: 4)

44

Jaci Maraschin of the Brazilian Episcopal Anglican Church while advocating contextualization of liturgy has warned that

> Any liturgical reform should be related to mission and should be based in a new theology relating mission to joy and freedom. Liturgy and mission are sisters dancing together in the direction of the beauty of the kingdom of God. (Douglas and Pui-Lan: 2001, 336)

The *New World Liturgy* and the *Workers' Mass* are two responses to social change and challenges to the Church's mission agenda. They are products of their times and need to be re-evaluated for their role and impact today, but they are none the less two excellent examples of alternative contextualization of liturgy in Sri Lanka.

Endnotes

1. For example, A confession in the penitential liturgy:
We are here because we are human, but we deny our humanity. We do not love others. We fail our fellows and dodge the truth about ourselves. We war against life. We hurt each other. We are sorry for it and know we are sick from it. We seek new life.
Giver of life, heal us and free us to be human.
Holy Spirit, speak to us. Help us to understand for we are dense. Come fill this moment. (The Workers' Mass: 6)
4. The text from the Upanishads beginning the Ministry of the Word:
OM...
With our ears may we hear what is good
With our eyes may we behold your righteousness
Tranquil in body may we who worship you find rest
OM...Shanthi – Shanthi – Shanthi. (1993: 8)
5. O God, the King of righteousness, lead us, we pray thee, in the ways of justice and of peace, inspire us to break down all tyranny and oppression, to gain for every man his due reward and from every man his due service; that each may live for all and all may care for each, in the name of Jesus Christ
6. Words at the peace are:
As we offer you + this Agni and + incense Lord, Renew your creation and reconcile us.
Fill us all with the fire and sweetness of your love.
Beloved, let us love one another for love is of God.
7. There is no prayer of thanksgiving, blessing, dismissal or closing hymn as those who framed the WM firmly believed that Reception is the climax of the Liturgy. The workers, nourished by their participation in the Liturgy, go out to engage in their various tasks to the glory of God, the good of all human beings and to continue their struggle for transformative justice

5

Examples of Contextualization in Current Liturgies

Narme Francis Wickremesinghe

Introduction

St. Paul writes "To the Jews I became like a Jew to win the Jews. To those under the law, I became like one under the law.... so as to win those under the law... I do it all for the sake of the gospel" (*1 Cor.9:20, 23*). It is on this basis that the current Liturgies in the Church of Ceylon have given options for the use of indigenous national customs. This is a part of the Church's missiological imperative, the interaction of worship and culture, and also a dialogue of Gospel and culture (Tovey, 2004, 2; Atta-Bafoe and Tovey, 1990, 14).

In Sri Lanka there are two main languages and cultures. After the colonisation of the country by the British, the missionaries seemed to have made a definite attempt to prevent the practice of the local culture, customs and festivals amongst the local converts to Christianity. Until the autonomy of the Church of Ceylon in 1930 and National Independence in 1948 generations of Sri Lankan Anglicans were alienated from 90% of their citizens and even now middle class urban Christians in Sri Lanka seem to think that attempts at contextualization is syncretism with other religions (Atta-Bafoe and Tovey, 1990: 15). For instance, *urban* Christians generally do not celebrate the National New Year in April (saying it is Buddhist and Hindu).

The first three Sri Lankan Anglican Bishops emphasised that *we are not only Sri Lankan Christians: we are also Christian Sri Lankans* (Wickremesinghe, 2017, 30; Billimoria, 2016, 227,229). Contextualization of the Liturgy, in Sri Lanka is done with an Asian liberation theology and local culture approach as exemplified by the New World Liturgy and Workers Mass (England, 1986, 277-28; Devananda, 1968, 32-43; see chapter 4). The current Liturgies of the Church of Ceylon – the Eucharist (2013), Baptism (2013), Marriage (2016), Funerals (2016), Healing & Reconciliation (2016) have their provenance in similar Christian Workers' Fellowship (CWF) Liturgies but in a less radical way to enable wider acceptance in the parishes. Sinhala and Tamil cultures and customs have optionally been allowed to enable Anglicans to be one with the rest of the people of Sri Lanka but with a Christian meaning to the national tradition. Compilers of contextual Liturgies in Sri Lanka have been influenced by the statement in 1956 of Bishop Lakdasa De Mel, the first Sri Lankan Anglican Bishop and last Metropolitan of India (CIPBC):

> the early Church was incredibly daring in baptising the national culture into Christ… man's religion had to enter into his environment and culture, taking over places, seasons and customs associated with pre-Christian religious observances and with inspired intuition turning them to Christian profit… he who fears to make a mistake ends by making nothing…The wide accommodating charity of primitive days has given way to self-conscious dread of syncretism which testifies to the lack of spiritual powers within (De Mel, 1956 cited in Wickremesinghe 2017, 27 & 28).

The Liturgy of Holy Baptism for Sri Lanka (2013)
The Baptismal Liturgy of the Church of Ceylon together with 'Notes On Entry Into The Church' is given in *Anglican Baptismal Liturgies* (Tovey, 2017, 234 – 242). Its Structure is based on the IALC Toronto Statement (Holeton, 1993, 252); its Corporate Nature and words are based on the *'Baptism, Eucharist and Ministry'* document (WCC, 1982) and the

example of an Ecumenical Baptismal Liturgy (Thurian and Wainwright, 1983, 94-96); and its Richly Holistic cultural symbolism derived from local birth customs (Wickremesinghe, 2017, 110) used in the CWF Baptismal Liturgy (Wickremesinghe, 1993, 213).

Certain principles of initiation (Holeton, 1993, 229) are given in the 'Notes On Entry':

1) Baptism marks the entry into the One, Holy, Catholic and Apostolic Church.

2)Holy Baptism is *full and complete sacramental initiation* into the Christian community commanded by Christ, by water and the Holy Spirit in the name of the Father and of the Son and of the Holy Spirit.

3) Baptism is given once for life, and being a calling and gift of God is *unrepeatable* and irrevocable (Rom. 11:29).

4) The theology and ritual of Holy Baptism is common both to infants and adults and expressed by a common Liturgical Order.

5) Confirmation, Reception and Renewal are various modes of response to Baptism, each directly related to the one Covenant (Eph. 4: 4-6) made in Baptism and should consequently take place primarily in the context of the Liturgy of Baptism (Wickremesinghe, 1993 216) and at which the congregation too renews its Baptismal commitment and undertakes to nurture the new Christian in the Lord.

The Baptism is directed to take place in full view and participation of the congregation after the sermon in the Eucharist on Sunday. An adult candidate may give a testimony after the sermon. Commenting on the stages of Baptism in the New Testament period prior to AD 100, Johnson says "the proclamation of the Gospel leads to some kind of response of faith" (Johnson, 2007, 45).

First the parents and spiritual parents (or adult candidates by themselves) make a presentation of those to be Baptised acknowledging God's own initiative and Christ's call and requesting Christian nurture.

Then the Presider says either an extempore or formal prayer embodying national birth customs and giving its Christian meaning, e.g.: oiling of the body with gingelly oil (a Tamil cleansing custom depicting the cleansing power of the Holy Spirit), reminiscent of pre-baptismal anointing in the early church (Johnson, 2007, 123, 127; Baldwin, 1989, 17; McGowan, 2014, 156), striking with an ekel of a coconut leaf for protection and health / exorcism, a Sinhala custom and marking a *thilaka or pottuwa* (forehead mark among Sri Lankan babies and Tamil adults) with sandalwood and salt paste, symbolic of God's protection and the spreading fragrance of a Christian example.

The Thanksgiving over the water follows, beginning with a Christianized version of the commencement of worship in other national religions: "Homage to the One God, the Ultimate Reality (Logos) – That You Are (Ex.3:14): The Father, The Son and The Holy Spirit. **Amen**" The prayer continues in giving thanks for the qualities of water and the Spirit and to its allusions in the Bible ending with an *epiklesis* over those to be Baptised in this water. During the prayer, salt (of the earth) may be added and olive oil hallowed (seal of the Holy Spirit). Then there is the threefold renunciation followed by a confession in the form of the Eastern *Trisagion*. The declaration of faith follows. One of the alternative declarations is the Triple Refuge which is a Christianized version of a popular Buddhist chant:

> I take refuge in you Parent God
> I take refuge in you Christ Lord
> I take refuge in you blest Spirit
> I take refuge in you Three as one God
> (Tovey, 2017, 238)

A lock of hair is cut from the crown of the head of an infant in symbolism of a first visit to a religious place. The triple pouring of water on the head or immersion in the case of adults is made with the Presbyter saying the

Baptismal formula in its passive words as done by the first Christians to visit Sri Lanka in the sixth Century (Persian – East Syrian Rite):

N. is Baptised in the name of the Father and of the Son and of the Holy Spirit. **Amen**

It indicates that Baptism is by God alone, collectively done by the Church as a whole in a Liturgical Rite. Then the Presider may make the consignation with olive oil (or Chrism) and lay hands on the head claiming the candidate for Christ and calling the Holy Spirit to enable mission, saying:

N. receive the Seal of the gift of the Holy Spirit: may it make you a faithful witness to the Christ of God. **Amen**

The Church of Ceylon has followed what is done in the neighbouring Christian East (the Indian Malabar Orthodox Church, the Mar Thoma Church, the Byzantine Rite) and as well as a practice of antiquity in North Africa, and Syria (Whitaker, 2003, 9, 13, 36, 39, 94-95; Johnson, 2007, 127-134, 299). As Johnson argues the *single* post Baptismal anointing should never simply be equated with Western Confirmation. However, in an Episcopal Baptism of an adult in Sri Lanka the Confirmation takes place at this point with these same words.

At Baptism we have been buried with Christ into death and raised with Christ into newness of life (c.f. Rom. 6:3). Thus, in Reception or Renewal there is a circumambulation around the place of Baptism three times, a cultural symbolism of death and new life.

Finally the newly baptized are clothed in a white garment (Gal. 3:7) and given a lighted earthenware lamp (Eph. 5:4) – ancient and current symbolism of enlightenment / illumination (Johnson 2007, 38; McGowan 2014, 149) and being sent out as lights of the world (Tovey, 2015, 10). Note that lighted clay lamps and white clothes are used in religious places in Sri Lanka indicating enlightenment and purity (regeneration). They are then welcomed by the Lay Officers of the Parish as "*full* members of the Church liberated to a new humanity" and with a round of applause. From the time of the Didache' (circa.100) Baptism was the only qualification to receive the Eucharist. Although this is implied by the Sri Lankan Rite and the Constitution (Chapter 24 Canons 2 and 15) it is hardly ever practiced without Episcopal Confirmation.

In relation to the Eucharist that follows the newly baptised or confirmed and their spiritual parents gets involved actively in the Greeting of Peace and the Taking. A national feature is the offering of milk rice, buffalo milk curd and honey for consumption after the service. These foods are consumed during joyful national celebrations. It is reminiscent of milk and honey consumed at the Eucharist as described in antiquity. (Johnson, 2007, 100, 111).

The contextual Baptismal Service was described in detail to give the western reader an idea that official Services in Sri Lanka though keeping to an established model intends to bring in the culture and soul of the Sri Lankan psyche to those who so desire it.

Ordinations (2013)

The Sri Lankan Ordinal is included in Phillip Tovey's *Anglican Ordination Rites*, (2019). Since 1990 Sri Lanka has adapted the Ordination Services of the 1989 A New Zealand Prayer Book. In 2013 it adopted the General Principles and Elements of the Ordination Rite given in the 2001 IALC Berkeley Statement (Gibson, 2002, 11-17). For purposes of brevity only the contextualization in the Episcopal Ordination will be considered here but it is common to all Ordination Rites. All Ordinations are trilingual (i.e. in Sinhala, Tamil and English) and the music and traditions from all ethnicities are utilized.

National and other religious events in Sri Lanka begin with processions[1] led by drummers, flautists, and national dancers. So also, the processions in Anglican Ordinations – an act of worship, a sign of the Church in pilgrimage with the clergy and laity in a walk together binding them to Christ, an intersection of liturgy and mission (Gordon-Taylor & Jones, 2008, 19-20). The Bishop-elect / Ordinands will walk through the adult baptismal pool with water at the entrance to the Cathedral, and process to the front of the congregation and take their seats with the family and presenters. This is to show that Baptism is the root of all Christian Ministry and Calling (1997 Javenpaa Interim IALC in Holeton, (1997), para 1, 14, 30 & 48).

The final procession of the Ordaining Bishops takes place to the chant of the Litany for Ministry in a local pilgrim chant tune inside the Cathedral. This is the pilgrim chant tune used in national Buddhist pilgrimages up Adam's Peak (called Sri-Pada or Blessed Feet Mountain), Christianized by the street processional Litany on May Day of the CWF. The Litany ends with a sung *Kyrie* confession in a local language. The presentation is done by representative men and women. The process of the Ordination is within a specific Christian community (Bradshaw, 2006, 219-220; 1997, 9).

It is followed by the Ministry of the Word. The Ordinands / Bishop-elect then takes leave of their parents / families by touching their toes – the national way of greeting elders. The next section of Declaration of Episcopal functions, Examination, Prayer and Laying on of hands is called in the Sri Lankan Liturgy 'The Liturgy of Higher (Episcopal) Ordination', reminiscent of a similar term used in the majority religion in Sri Lanka. There is a long silence as the congregation prays while the candidate prostrates before God. After a lyric to the Holy Spirit the whole congregation stretches out a hand, the ordaining Bishops stand to pray led by the Vicar General, while two Bishops hold a Bible opened at John 20:22 'Receive the Holy Spirit' over the nape of the neck of the Bishop elect (*Apostolic Constitution VIII*, 4, 6) symbolising that it is Christ who ordains and the other Bishops scrum down to lay hands. A significant feature in Sri Lanka is that Heads of other Christian Churches *later join the Bishops in continuing the Ordination prayer*, laying hands and quoting 2Tim.1:6-7 & John 20:22. In the next part of the prayer a Bishop (often from the Mar Thoma Church) anoints the new Bishop saying the Orthodox ordination prayer:

> Divine grace which always heals that which is infirm
> And completes what is lacking,
> empower *N* to be Bishop
> through the seal of the Holy Spirit
> (c.f. Bradshaw, 2014, 86; 2006, 221)

Then the final part of the prayer is said by the congregation. Thus, the whole community was involved in the prayers (Bradshaw, 1997, 10 - 11).

A Bible is given as a sign of authority and guidance. He or she is then vested in a cope. The traditional brass oil lamp is lit by the new Bishop and the Area Deans signifying the Sri Lankan tradition of a new beginning and undertaking to be the light of Christ (Matt. 5:14, John 8:12).

The Bishop then moves to the Holy Table or the Presiding Seat where he is given the insignia of a ring, pectoral cross and mitre. After the Installation the previous Diocesan Bishop hands over the Diocesan pastoral staff. The new Bishop then washes the feet of 12 persons from the Diocese. All Bishops and heads of Christian Churches then present the Bishop to the Congregation in these words: "People of the Diocese of ... you have a new Bishop, *N.*" There is then a celebratory rolling of local drums and blowing of conch shells together with a spontaneous applause. The exchange of the Peace between the new Bishop and the other Bishops and the congregation brings the Ordination to a close and begins the Eucharist.

Marriage Services (Experimental 2016)
The Marriage Service is intended to be done with the Eucharist but often is done alone. The 'deep structures' of the Cranmerian Rite (consent and blessing) remain but as in the Christian East the Rite is based around the Liturgy of the Word and the stress on celebration (Stevenson, 2011, 21,

24, 13) with the optional use of much cultural symbolism and climaxing in the blessing. In every Section there is an emphasis on community, Trinity and the concept of marriage as a gift (Lloyd, 2013, 173). The response in the consent is in the present tense and Hollywood 'I do' not 'I will' (Cooper, 2011, 42).

Among the 5 alternate nuptial blessings are the 16 Tamil Blessings of Life, the adapted 7 Hebrew Benedictions (as an antecedent to Christian Marriage) and the traditional 8-fold Sinhala Blessings (only in the Sinhala BCP 1995, 320).[2]

There is also a Form of Blessing of a Civil Marriage for mixed faith marriages and divorcees quoting 1 Cor. 7:14, necessary in a country where only around 6% of the population is Christian. Marriages are occasions where many in the congregation are not Christians and the provision of cultural customs and the Word is part of the contextualization of the Liturgy and mission.

The following optional symbolism in the Marriage Service indicates the need for rehearsals (Farrimond, 2007, 97-98):

1. In both the Sinhala and Tamil cultures the bridegroom and then the bride are escorted to a canopied podium (Sinhala *Poruwa* and Tamil *Manavarai)*. Baptismal water is asperged on the couple by the Presbyter. This canopied podium has been in use in Sri Lanka from a time before the advent of Buddhism but developed during British colonialism as a competitive equivalent to the Christian Marriage ceremony (Somaratne, 2006, 61-83).

2. Prior to being conducted to the podium at the entrance to the Church the bridegroom's feet may be washed by a male relative of a Sinhala bride, a token of unreserved acceptance into the bride's family. Among Tamils, each partner is received and garlanded *(Isa.61:10)* by the other partner's parents or family and the couple made to sit on the ground in the podium facing each other.

3. The clergy begin the service with the exhortation on marriage. It

is followed by a prayer, the consent and the Ministry of the Word. After the homily is the confession – a rarity in traditional Anglican weddings. Like in Judaism it could be considered as the day when the past sins of the couple are forgiven and they merge into a new complete soul as one.

4. Seven betel leaves (Botanical name – *Piper betle*) are dropped on the ground during the confession and vows symbolic of repentance and the vows being witnessed by God's created earth and generations of the couple's ancestors (Vundla, 1990, 36). It symbolises the creation of a new world by the couple and the wholeness (depicted by 7) that they cannot attain separately. Each Promise is taken before a fire (Tamil custom), but for Christians symbolic of the Holy Spirit.

5. Before taking the promises the bridegroom and the bride fall at the feet of their parents / maternal uncle and take their leave, and the bridegroom greets the bride's parents with a sheaf of betel leaves – a national custom of respect.

6. After the vows two rings, *thali* (Tamil wedding necklace), toe ring and going away saree may be placed on a Holy Bible, symbolic of all belongings coming from God *(1 Chron. 29:14b)* and hallowed. A Tamil custom is to take all ornament on a tray to the midst of the congregation to be blessed with uplifted hands or throwing small flowers. In both cultures a necklace is fastened by the bridegroom around the neck of the bride as a token of marriage. Amongst the Sinhala people the rings are placed on the fourth finger of the *left* hand of each other while in the Tamil culture the rings are placed on the index finger of the *right* hands.

7. After the exchange of rings the Presbyter ties the small fingers of the couple (bride's right and bridegroom's left) with a gold thread (purity) and then pours baptismal water over the fingers symbolising the eternal unity of the couple and of different Christian Churches in Holy Baptism and in the local tradition of water and the earth on which it falls being eternal verities, a lasting witness to the marriage.

8. 'The central act of the wedding service' is the *Nuptial Blessing / Crowning*. ("In the crown with which his mother has crowned him on the day of his marriage.... " *Sg.of Sgs.3:11*). They may be anointed during the blessing. After the blessing, the newlyweds may garland each other and light a single lamp symbolic of beginning one family. Like the Hebrew breaking of a glass of wine to mark the end of the wedding ceremony an Uncle may break a coconut, symbolic of annihilating egoism.

On important occasions Buddhist festive stanzas called *Jayamangala Gatha* are sung as a blessing. These are joyous victory verses recalling the Lord Buddha's victory over his powerful opponents defeating evil with virtue. It is sung at Sinhala Weddings as a blessing on the couple. The equivalent Christianized stanzas in the Anglican Marriage Service are sung to the same traditional tune and when translated is as follows:

The Lord over sits on high / by Angels adored
By Father, Son, Spirit – the world is protected
Now reigns the Triune God / in the highest heaven
May you by God's glory / receive divine blessing.

In the marriage of Cana when / all the wine was over
Christ provided the wine / to help the beloved mother
The divine Son, love of love /ever reigns on high
May you by Christ's glory / receive divine blessing.

Shattering the mighty power / of grim death and grave
Victorious Christ rose again / the whole world to save
The fearless divine spirit / now with us stays
May you by the Spirit's glory / receive divine blessing.

Funeral Services (Experimental 2016)

The Introduction to the Church of Ceylon Funeral Services states "In the Sri Lankan context families are closely knit and the death of a loved one has an impact on the lives of those who remain --- as they grieve through denial (numbness), anger (irritable), bargaining (if...), depression and finally coming to terms with the loss and resolving the grief.... the services should not be too long and here includes some cultural, traditional and historical elements and flexibility must be utilised according to circumstances".

The Funeral Services are more a resource book for the Minister to select prayers, biblical sentences and readings from Commendation of the dying, through the Service at home or funeral parlour, Service in Church with or without the Eucharist, cemetery or crematorium Service, burial of ashes, and the funeral of a child to Services of Thanksgiving & Remembrance. The process from dying to memorial is like a journey, along which the Church should offer support at different stages (Lloyd, 2012, 10). As the Notes say "these services need not be done exactly in the form given and flexibility with extempore prayer is encouraged".

In these Funeral Services like elsewhere in Anglicanism the pattern is inherited from the 1662 Book of Common Prayer (2007 IALC Palermo Statement in Lloyd, 2012, 11) but borrowing much from *Common Worship 2000*. In Sri Lanka funerals are occasions when any person known to the deceased or the family members will culturally attend the layout (wake) or funeral. Hence it is important that Christian teachings on death and resurrection are incorporated into the funeral rite as a missiological emphasis while adapting cultural practices and symbols giving specifically Christian meanings (Farrimond, 20017, 96: Lloyd, 2012, 15). Significantly unlike many African Rites (e.g. Nigeria 1966, Kenya 2002) the Notes in Sri Lanka are silent on the social context of whether the deceased is not baptized, excommunicated or suicidal death, but obviously for those having a Christian background. This is to provide for wide pastoral considerations of the living at a time of severe shock and grief. Also unlike at the Reformation there are options of prayers for the dead e.g. 'Go forth upon your journey', 'Into your hands we commend' and the *Russian Kontakion* for the dead (Larson-Miller, 2013, 181, 185).

At the reception of the body in the Church or cemetery the coffin and the persons around may be sprinkled with baptismal water linking the funeral to Baptism (Larson-Miller, 2013, 187; Farrimond, 2007, 108). Sprinkling the coffin with small flowers depicting life is a local symbol. The procession from the gate or Church door led by the Paschal Candle represents the power of the risen Christ over death and Christian hope, as well as the journey through the liminal door way where, in funerals the separation stage predominates (Farrimond, 2007, 94). The Introduction to the Funeral Services give these stages for both the dead person and the family to be like Christ's Good Friday, Holy Saturday and Easter: Chaos and separation at death, the liminality of transition during the Funeral Rites, and finally the incorporation into eternal life for the deceased and then to the family a new life without the deceased.

Either before the removal of the body from home or at the cemetery there is an option called 'The Commendation and Farewell' replacing the former 'Office of the Dead'. It begins with "We shall all be changed" (1 Cor. 15:51-53) and merges with the optional cultural ceremony of the relatives pouring water in to a cup until it overflows (signifying abundant consolation through Christ 2 Cor. 1:5) whilst the following cultural stanzas (or alternative commendatory prayers) are said –

By *N*.'s life and faith and being justified by our Mediator, The Lord Jesus Christ, s/he has attained peace. Amen.

Just as the rivers filled with water by rain flow into the sea and fill it, so has *N*.'s life of faith through the merits of our Saviour the Lord Jesus Christ filled his / her soul. Amen.

Just as the rain water flows from higher elevation to a lower elevation and just as smoke rises to the sky, may our prayers with that of the faithful departed and the Saints and Angels flow to the throne of heavenly grace and be accepted on high. Amen.

The equivalent stanzas in Buddhism seek to bring merit to wondering unsettled souls of the dead relative (*preta*) (De Silva, 1974, 87).

Whilst the adapted traditional stanzas or commendations are said the Presider will burn sweet smelling joss sticks or incense around the bier. He will then use the water in the cup to asperge the bier and the congregation as a reminder of our common one baptism to the one Church of the One Lord (*Eph. 4:4*). However, it must be stated that Christians in practice rarely use this national cultural ceremony and it has been included in the Funeral Services for those mourners who wish to integrate with the Nation's culture.

The liturgical colour for funerals in Sri Lanka is off-white, an inheritance from the Asian culture. Funerals are reminders of the resurrection (white) and eternal life (Wickremesinghe, 2017, 146). Black is never used in other religious places in Sri Lanka although Anglicans continue to use black scarves (tippet) at Evensong and Roman Catholic and Christian laity often wear black at funerals.

Calendar & Lectionary

The Calendar and Lectionary for Sri Lanka is another significant example of contextualization (Billimoria, 2016, 226). It enables the Church to join the Nation in commemorations for National Independence Day (04 February), Tamil Thai Pongal or Sinhala New Rice Festival (harvest, 14 January), National New Year (14 April), National Heros' Day (22 May), National Tree Planting day (17 September), Lord Buddha (Full Moon day in May), Prophet Mohamed (27 August) etc,. Additionally there are days or Sundays that enable a remembrance of the history of the Church in Sri Lanka such as Church of Ceylon Day / Sunday (08 July 1886 – beginning of Synodical Government), Saints of our Diocese (07 November 1845 – foundation of the first Diocese then involving the whole of Sri Lanka).

Another peculiarity of the Sri Lankan calendar are commemorations of Old Testament Prophets with paired dating 6 months before as in Ancient Jerusalem (Baldovin, 1989, 43) e.g. Elijah (19 July same date as in Israel, paired with unity week), Jeremiah (02 August, paired with the Presentation), Isaiah (06 July paired with the Epiphany) and Zechariah (26 June paired with St Stephen).

Conclusion

The Church of Ceylon Liturgical Committee has experimented courageously with the truth, for the God who loves also forgives. It has boldly provided for those who so opt to be one with the culture of the majority of the people of Sri Lanka without fear of syncretism and like the early Church baptised the national culture into Christ (See Introduction above). However, the majority of urban Sri Lankan Christians have grown up in what Billimoria quoting John Pobee calls 'Anglo Saxon captivity' (Billimoria, 2016, 230: Sykes and Booty, 1988, 394). Thus, in urban areas these optional provisions for cultural customs are not used often. Further, usage of these customs in Anglican Services need rehearsals and busy Clergy do not even inform parents and couples of the availability of authorised cultural provisions. As the young urban Anglicans associate more and more with their counterparts in other religions in daily life, these cultural customs may have a wider acceptance in the future and "overcome cultural alienation" (Tovey, 2004, 3).

Let me end by quoting Bishop Duleep de Chickera

Worship in the Church of Ceylon is solemn and participatory and includes cultural elements such as drumming, dancing, indigenous lyrics, the prostration, use of the rotti or chapathi as the host, and the lighting of the traditional oil lamp. Clergy preside barefooted; and sesath (colourful banners on colourful poles which symbolize the presence of the monarchy) are carried in liturgical processions and adorn the sanctuary to indicate that worship is directed to Christ the King. In some congregations and on special occasions such ordinations worship is trilingual. In many congregations it is bi-lingual. Music is provided from either an organ or eastern instruments such as the tabla, serapina and sitar. Contemporary feature in the Canon of the Eucharist is the reference to "Sages" along with the Law and the Prophets as vehicles of God's revelation to humans. (De Chickera, 2013, 365)

Endnotes

1. Locally called perahara e.g. the famous Kandy Esala Perahara
2. The Christianized 16 Blessings of life is as follows:

O Triune God grant them Aesthetic Gifts!
O Triune God grant them Valour!
O Triune God grant them Success!
O Triune God grant them Virtuous Children!
O Triune God grant them Courage!
O Triune God grant them Wealth!
O Triune God grant them Rice!
O Triune God grant them Happy Life!
O Triune God grant them Joys of Life!
O Triune God grant them Wisdom!
O Triune God grant them Beauty!
O Triune God grant them New Achievements!
O Triune God grant them Righteous Life!
O Triune God grant them Family Fame!
O Triune God grant them Health!
O Triune God grant them Long Life!

Bibliography

Abayasekera, J. (2002). *Bishop Lakdasa De Mel: Called for justice and uplift of poor* https://web.archive.org/web/20150924111814/http://www.sundayobserver.lk/2002/10/27/fea08.html, (Accessed 24 *May 2019*).

Abayasekera. J. (2016). *Sevaka Yohan Devananda*. http://www.island.lk/index.php?page_cat=article-details&page=article-details&code_title=145210 (Accessed 24 May 2019).

Anon, (1927), 'Notes and Comments: Prayer Book Revision', *Theology*, Vol. 14, No. 31, March 1927, 165-167.

Ariarajah, S. W. (2018). *Moving Beyond the Impasse: Reorienting Ecumenical and Interfaith Relations*. Minneapolis: Fortress Press.

Atta Bafoe, V. R. and Tovey, P. (1990). 'What Does Inculturation Mean', in Holeton, David. R (ed.), *Liturgical Inculturation in the Anglican Communion*. JLS 15, Nottingham: Grove Books.

Balding. J.W., (1922). *One Hundred Years in Ceylon, or, The Centenary Volume of the Church Missionary Society in Ceylon, 1818-1918*. Madras: The Diocesan Press.

Baldovin, J. F, (1989). *Liturgy in Ancient Jerusalem*, JLS 9, Nottingham: Grove Books.

Bevan, F. L. (1946). *A History of the Diocese of Colombo*. Colombo: Diocese of Colombo.

Billimoria, M. (2015). 'Sri Lanka', in Chapman, M. (et al.) *The Oxford Handbook of Anglican Studies*, Oxford: OUP.

Blomfield, J. (1930). *The Eucharistic Canon*, London: SPCK.

Bradshaw, P. (1997). 'Ordination as God's Action through the Church', in Holeton, D. R. (ed.), *Anglican Orders and Ordinations*, JLS 39, Cambridge: Grove Books.

Bradshaw, P. (2006). 'Ordination Services', in Bradshaw, P. (ed.,), *A Companion to Common Worship*, Volume 2, London: SPCK.

Bradshaw, P. F. (2014). *Rites of Ordination – Their History and Theology*, London: SPCK.

Buchanan, C. (1993). 'Confirmation', in Holeton, D. R, (ed.), *Growing in Newness of Life*, Toronto: Anglican Book Centre.

Buchanan, C. (1997). 'Anglican Orders and Unity', in Holeton, D. R, (ed.), *Anglican Orders and Ordinations*, JLS 39, Cambridge: Grove Books.

Buchanan, C. (2014). *Baptism as Complete Sacramental Initiation* W 219, Cambridge: Grove Books.

Buchanan, C.O. (1975). *Further Anglican Liturgies*, Bramcote: Grove Books.

Celebrating Surya Sena's musical endeavour with the Sinhala Liturgy, The Sunday Times, Sunday April 19, 2015, http://www.sundaytimes.lk/150419/plus/celebrating-surya-senas-musical-endeavour-with-the-sinhala-liturgy-145115.html (Accessed 2019).

Chapman, M. D., Clarke, S. & Percy, M. (eds.) (2016). *The Oxford Handbook of Anglican Studies*. Oxford: OUP.

Christ Church, Baddegama, Church of Ceylon Diocese of Colombo, https://www.dioceseofcolombo.lk/97-churches/galle-archdeconry/205-christ-church-baddegama (Accessed 2019).

Christian Workers' Fellowship (1984). *For A Real Sri Lankan Church*. Colombo: CWF.

Christian Workers' Fellowship (6th Revision 1991/1992, Reprinted 1993). *Workers' Mass*. Colombo: CWF.

Church of Ceylon (1988). *The Holy Eucharist or The Lord's Supper*, Ratmalana: Deaf School Press.

Church of Ceylon (1997). *The Holy Eucharist – The Lord's Supper*, [Colombo: Church of Ceylon].

Church of Ceylon (2013). *The Holy Eucharist – The Lord's Supper*, Colombo: Unie Arts (PVT) Ltd.

Cooper, T. (2011). 'Wilt Thou Have This Women? – Asking God's Blessing on Consenting Adults', in Stevenson K. W. (ed.), Anglican Marriage Rites, A Symposium, JLS 71, Norfolk Norwich: Hymns Ancient and Modern.

De Chickera, D. (2013). The Church of Ceylon (Extra-Provincial to the Archbishop of Canterbury), in Markham, I.S. (et al.) The Wiley-Blackwell Companion to the Anglican Communion, Chichester: Wiley-Blackwell.

De Mel, L. (1955). 'Experiments in Ceylon', The Ecumenical Review, 8, No. 1, Oct. 1955, 37.

De Mel, L. (1956). The Christian Liturgy in Ceylon, Hale Memorial Sermon, http://anglicanhistory.org/asia/lk/demel_liturgy1956.html (Accessed 2019).

De Silva, K. M. (1981). A History of Sri Lanka. Los Angeles: University of California Press.

De Silva, L. (1974). *Buddhism – Beliefs and Practices in Sri Lanka*, Battaramulla: SIOLL.

De Soysa, Harold (ed.) (1945). *The Church of Ceylon: Her Faith and Mission*. (Colombo: Diocese of Colombo).

Department of Census and Statistics, (2011). *Sri Lanka Census of Population and Housing*, http://www.statistics.gov.lk/PopHouSat/CPH2011/Pages/Activities/Reports/CPH_2012_5Per_Rpt.pdf, (Accessed 23 May 2019).

Deraniyagala, S. U. (2014). Pre and Protohistoric settlement in Sri Lanka. *International Union of Prehistoric and Protohistoric Sciences XIII U. I. S. P. P.* https://www.archaeology.lk/wp-content/uploads/2018/04/Prehistory_and_protohistory_of_Sri_Lanka.pdf (Accessed 23 May 2019).

Devananda, Y. (1968). *If They Had Met*, Devasaranaramaya NWP, Colombo: Wesley Press.

Devar Surya Sena (1941). *A Sinhalese Setting of the Ceylon Liturgy*, SPCK: Ceylon.

Devar Surya Sena (1945). 'Sinhalese Music in Church Worship', in de Soysa, H. *The Church of Ceylon her Faith and*

Bibliography

Mission, Colombo: Daily News Press, 187-189.

Devasarana Collective Farm (1973, Revised 1979). *New World Liturgy*, Ibbagamuwa: DCF.

Diocese of Colombo, (2015). *History of the Church of Ceylon Diocese of Colombo*. https://www.dioceseofcolombo.lk/diocese/history, (Accessed 24 May 2013).

Diocese of Kurunagala (2019). *History*. http://www.dioceseofkurunegala.com/history_of_kurunegala_diocese.php, (Accessed 24 May 2019).

Dornberg, U. (1992). *Searching Through the Crisis: Christians, Social Change in Sri Lanka in the 1970s and 1980s*. Colombo: Logos

Douglas, I. T. and Pui-Lan, Kwok (2001). *Beyond Colonial Anglicanism: The Anglican Communion in the Twenty-First Century*. New York: Church Publishing Incorporated.

England, J. C, (1986). 'Indigenization', in Davis J.C. (ed.), *Dictionary of Liturgy and Worship*, 1st ed. London: SCM Press.

Evans, G. R. and Wright, J. R. (1991). *The Anglican Tradition*. London: SPCK.

Fabella, V. and Sugirtharajah, R. S. (eds.) (2003). *The SCM Dictionary of Third World Theologies*. London: SCM Press.

Fernando. K. (2009). *Integrity and Integration of Christian Community in Sri Lanka*. Colombo: S. Godage and Brothers.

Ferrinand, S. (2007). 'Weddings and Funerals', in Irvine, C. (ed.), *The Use and Symbols of Worship*, Alcuin Liturgy Guide 4, London: SPCK.

Gibson, P. (2002). *Anglican Ordination Rites – The Berkeley Statement: 'To Equip the Saints'*, W 168 Cambridge: Grove Books.

Gordon-Taylor, B. and Jones, S. (2008). *Celebrating Christ's Appearing*, Alcuin Liturgy Guide 5, London: SPCK.

Griffiths, D.N. (2002). *The Bibliography of the Book of Common Prayer 1549-1999*, London: the British Library.

Harris, E. (2016). 'Art, Liturgy and the Transformation of Memory: Christian Rapprochement with Bhuddism in Post-Independence Sri Lanka', *Religions of South Asia*, 10.1 pp 50-78.

Hinchliff, P. (1959). *The South African Liturgy*, Cape Town: OUP.

Holeton, D. R. (1989). *Findings of the Third International Anglican Consultation*, Bramcote: Grove Books.

Holeton, D. R., (1993). *Growing in Newness of Life*, Anglican Book Centre: Toronto.

Holeton, D.R. (ed.) (1990). *Liturgical Inculturation in the Anglican Communion*, JLS 15, Nottingham: Grove Books.

Jasper, R.C.D. (1954). *Walter Howard Frere. His Correspondence on Liturgical Revision and Construction*, Alcuin Club Collection No. 39, London: SPCK.

Jasper, R.C.D. (1989). *The Development of the Anglican Liturgy*, London: SPCK.

Jayasinghe, S (2015). '"Identity Crisis" of Post-Colonial Church Architecture in Sri Lanka', Research Gate, https://www.researchgate.net/publication/327419057.

Johnson, M. E. (2007). *The Rites of Christian Initiation, Its Evolution and Interpretation*, Minnesota: Liturgical Press.

Jones, S. (2016). *Celebrating Christian Initiation*, Alcuin Liturgy Guide 7, London: SPCK.

Jose, C.C., (1996). *Life and achievements of blessed Joseph Vaz: Apostle of Canara and Sri Lanka*. Sydney: Pilar Publications.

Karunarathna. M.(2002). *Rev. Lakdasa de Mel: Inspiring legend of Baddegama*.https://web.archive.org/web/20110604225909/http://www.dailynews.lk/2002/10/28/fea03.html, (Accessed 24 May 2019).

Kennedy, D. J. (2016). *Eucharistic Sacramentality in an Ecumenical Context: The Anglican Epiclesis*. Routledge: London & New York.

Larson-Miller, L. (2013). 'Death and Dying', in Day, J. and Gordon-Taylor, B. (eds.), *The Study of Liturgy and Worship*, Alcuin Liturgy Guide, London: SPCK.

Lloyd, T. (2000). *Dying and Death Step by Step, a Funeral Flow Chart*, W 160, Cambridge: Grove Books.

Lloyd, T. (2012). *Rites Surrounding Death, Commentary on the IALC 2007 Palermo Statement*, JLS 74, Norfolk Norwich: Hymns Ancient and Modern.

Lloyd, T. (2013). 'Marriage', in Day, J. and Gordon-Taylor, B. (eds.), *The Study of Liturgy and Worship*, Alcuin Liturgy Guide, London: SPCK.

Mahavansa.org (2007). *The Coming of Vijaya*. http://mahavamsa.org/mahavamsa/original-version/06-coming-vijaya/ (Accessed 23 May 2019).

Markham, I. S., (et al.) (eds.) (2013). *The Wiley-Blackwell Companion to the Anglican Communion*, Chichester: John Wiley & Sons.

Martin, D. and Mullen, P. (eds.) (1981). *No Alternative: The Prayer Book Controversy*. Oxford: Blackwell.

McGowan, A. B, (2014). *Ancient Christian Worship*, Grand Rapids: Baker Academics.

Meyers, R. A, (1988). 'The Structure of the Syrian Baptismal Rite', in Bradshaw, P. F. (ed.), *Essays in Early Eastern Initiation*, A/GLS 8, Nottingham: Grove Books.

Bibliography

National Christian Council of Sri Lanka (2014). *Jesus Christ Sri Lankan Expressions*, Colombo: National Christian Council of Sri Lanka.

Paranavithana, K. D. (2002). *Wolvendaal Church - Dutch Reformed Church in Sri Lanka - 360 years of history*. http://www.lankalibrary.com/geo/dutch/church.htm (Accessed 24 May2019).

Pinto, L. (2013). *A Brief History of Christianity In Sri Lanka*. https://www.colombotelegraph.com/index.php/a-brief-history-of-christianity-in-sri-lanka/ (Accessed 24 May 2019).

Sachs, William L. (ed.) (2018). *The Oxford History of Anglicanism, Volume V*. Oxford: OUP, 2018.

Somaratna, G.P.V. (1996). 'Christianity in Sri Lanka in the Anuradhapura Period', *Dharma Deepika*, Vol. 2, No. 2, 17-29.

Somaratne, G. P. V. (2006). *Sinhala Christian Worship*, Colombo: Colombo Theological Seminary.

Somaratne, G.P.V., (2006). *Marriage: Some Aspects of Buddhist Christian Encounter*, Colombo: Colombo Theological College.

Stevenson, K. and Spinks, B. (eds.) (1993). *The Identity of Anglican Worship*, London: Mowbray.

Stevenson, K. W, (2011). 'Setting the Scene: Background and Development', in Stevenson, K. W. (ed.), *Anglican Marriage Rites A Symposium*, JLS 71, Norfolk Norwich: Hymns Ancient and Modern.

Sykes, S. and Booty, J. (1988). *Study of Anglicanism*, London: SPCK.

The Ceylon Liturgy Committee, (1931). *An Order for the Administration of the Holy Communion* Wellawatte: Wesleyan Mission Press.

The Ceylon Liturgy Association, (1934). *An Order for a Requiem according to the Ceylon Liturgy*, [CLA: Colombo].

The Ceylon Liturgy Committee, (1932). *The Ceylon Liturgy: An Order for the Administration of the Holy Communion* Colombo: Freewin Printers.

The Ceylon Liturgy: An Order for the Administration of Holy Communion (1935). Madras: SPCK in India Burma and Ceylon

The Ceylon Liturgy: An Order for the Administration of Holy Communion (1938). Madras: SPCK in India Burma and Ceylon.

The Diocese of Kurunegala (1975). *Twenty-Five Years of the Dioceses of Kurunegala*. Kandy: Godamunne & Sons.

Thurian, M. and Wainwright, G. (1983). *Baptism and Eucharist, Ecumenical Convergence in Celebration*, WCC Faith and Order Paper 117, Geneva.

Tomb of King Duttagamani, Privy Stones. (1st ed.). Archeological Department (Ceylon): Colombo.

Tovey, P. (2004). *Inculturation of Christian Worship*, Aldershot: Ashgate.

Tovey, P. (2015). *Of Water and The Spirit*, Norwich: Canterbury Press.

Tovey, P. (2017). *Anglican Baptismal Liturgies*, Canterbury Press: Norwich.

Tovey, P. (2019). *Anglican Ordination Rites*, Amazon: Great Britain.

USPG (2016). *Liturgical Resources*. https://www.uspg.org.uk/docstore/146.pdf. (Accessed 24 May 2019).

Vazhuthanapally, J. (1988). *Archaeology of Mar Sliba*, OIRSI 139, Vadavathoor: Ruhalaya Publications.

Vidyasagara, Vijaya (2007). *Christian Ministry to the Workers: Challenges and Opportunities*, Colombo: Diocese of Colombo.

Vundla, T. J. (1990). 'Example Two: African Ancestors', In Holeton David. R (ed.), *Liturgical Inculturation in the Anglican Communion*, A/GLS 15, Nottingham: Grove Books.

W.K.L.C. (1933). 'The Ceylon Liturgy', *Theology*, Vol, 26, No. 152, Feb 1933, 101.

Whitaker, E.C. (2003). *Documents of the Baptismal Liturgy*, (3rd ed., Revised) Johnson, M. E., Alcuin Collection 79, London: SPCK

Wickremasinghe, N. (2011). 'Liturgy at the Synods/Council of the Colombo Diocese, in Diocese of Colombo', *Diocesan Council Salient Trends 1885-2010*, Colombo: Diocese of Colombo.

Wickremasinghe. N.F. (2017). *Being Anglican: Church of Ceylon*, Ratmalana: Hearing Impaired School Press.

Wickremesinghe, F. (1993). 'An Asian Inculturation of the Baptismal Liturgy', in Holeton, D. R. (ed.), *Growing in Newness of Life: Christian Initiation in Anglicanism Today*, Anglican Book Centre: Toronto.

Wickremesinghe, N.F, (2017). *Being Anglican – Church of Ceylon*, Deaf School Press: Ratmalana. (from www.vijithayapa.com).

Wiesbaden, O. (1983). 'Pali Literature'. in Gonda, J., (ed.), *A History of Indian Literature* Volume VII.1st ed. Germany: Kempton.

Wigan, B. (1964). *The Liturgy in English*, London: OUP.

Wingate, A., Ward, K., Pemberton, C. and Sitshebo, W. (eds.) (1998). *Anglicanism: A Global Communion*. London: Mowbray.

Wohlers, C. *The Book of Common Prayer. The Ceylon Liturgy*, http://justus.anglican.org/resources/bcp/India/ceylon.html (Accessed 2019)

World Council of Churches, (1982). *Baptism, Eucharist and Ministry*, Faith and Order Paper No: 111, Geneva.